1 Using a clear mid-green, stencil a leaf cluster, taking care not to overload your brush. For perfect stencilling, work the paint colour through the bristles, then 'stamp' off excess paint on a piece of rough paper. This way you will get soft, controlled colour with no risk of smudging.

2 Leaves as expressive as the ones that make up the Woodbine stencil gain enormously from shading here and there in different tones of green. Arrive at these by adding a little blue (for a cooler green) or raw umber (for a softer green) to your original colour. To shade, stipple colour on very lightly with a soft but firm bristled brush.

Stencilling is as easy as painting by numbers. Using fast-drying acrylic artists' colours, and either traditional straight-cut stencil brushes, or firm bristled artists' brushes as shown, follow our step-by-step instructions for perfect results.

CLIMBING ART

or Easy Steps to Perfect Stencilling

Keep equipment to a minimum to begin with: acrylic colours and bristle brushes available from any art shop, matt white emulsion paint (handy for softening and extending artists' colours), plus masking tape to hold the stencil in place, a plate for mixing colours, and a damp cloth for tidying up any mistakes.

ADD Twiddly tendrils reaching out for new supports are a very characteristic Woodbine feature, and this makes it easy to extend the design and give a sense of the plant's eagerly climbing growth. The twining growth makes it easy to extend or develop your stencilling in any direction, to suit your own room scheme and features.

FILL OUT 'Horses for courses' also applies to stencils; to fill a squarer space the elements need to be grouped together more compactly, as shown here. Try to keep a balance of colour between flowers and leaves for the most attractive effect.

3 Flowers can be stencilled in wherever they look right, once you have established the framework of Woodbine leaves and twining stems. Woodbine flowers belong to the Ipomea family, which include Morning Glories, so you can take your pick of colours from pure white, pink and white, or heavenly blue. Here we used pale, clear pink.

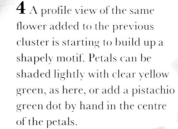

4 A profile view of the same flower added to the previous cluster is starting to build up a shapely motif. Petals can be shaded lightly with clear yellow green, as here, or add a pistachio green dot by hand in the centre of the petals.

BUILD Your stencilled Woodbine grows like the real thing, putting out new leading shoots and exploring tendrils. If you repeat the previous flowering group, you will begin to create a positive but informal and lively border. Our picture above shows the design both curved round into wreaths, and stencilled vertically as a border.

Wild flowers seem to look more at home on an airy and casual-looking painted finish. Here we have used a clear yellow Colourwash applied over a white emulsion base, to give a soft but sunny emphasis, especially valuable in dark or north-facing rooms.

NATURE ALL ENTWIN'D

Where to put your stencils is one of the first decisions to be made. They can be as symmetrical or as free-form as you choose. This low-ceilinged cottage room, with its odd little nooks and features, seems to call for an informal stencil treatment. Woodbine wanders prettily around a white painted plank door and up either side of a beam. Further tendrils encircling a plain card lampshade pick up the floral theme attractively. In a more conventional space, you might prefer to use the stencils more architecturally, underlining a cornice, or perhaps decorating the panels of a door. This would give a more composed effect.

Internal shutters, painted and stencilled, make an unusual and practical alternative to curtains at a small cottage window. In the daytime they can be folded right back to admit as much light as possible but, closed at night, the stencilled decoration comes into its own and gives a finished and cosy appearance, as well as keeping out the draughts. The Woodbine motif would look equally pretty stencilled on to a heavy cotton curtain, as a border design.

Shutters like these are a fairly simple DIY job: rectangles of sturdy plywood, with a flat moulding glued around the edges. Protect stencilled design with two coats of clear matt varnish.

A really junky firescreen can still be picked up for a pound or so in a jumble sale, and will look stunning when painted and stencilled to tone with your decor. Here, it gets a new lease of life with a background of soft yellow, and a stencilled wreath of flowering Woodbine.

NEW GROWTH ON OLD WOOD

It's Attention to Detail that Makes the Difference

Although we have chosen pretty, naturalistic colours for our Country Lanes stencils, this is only a starting point, and there is no reason why you should not experiment with the same designs in much bolder, 'fantasy' colours, as here. This is especially true of the woodbine design, where the stencilled shapes are strong and distinctive enough to carry a more dramatic colour scheme.

To show what a difference a change of colour scheme makes, we decorated this useful tray table in a pretty blue-green Crackleglaze. The striking texture of the crackled finish makes an unexpected background to the stencilled decoration, adding piquancy to a pink and white colour scheme which might otherwise have been too sweet. Crackled finishes are a favourite with professional decorative painters, but are now available in easy-to-use kit form. It is vital to protect the crackled surface with at least two coats of clear matt varnish.